Intelligence

Anthony Blake

By The Way Books
Sacramento, CA

First published in 1973 as "Intelligence Now"
Coombe Springs Press, Kingston, England
Reprinted several times

First By The Way Books edition
September 1999
Copyright © Anthony Blake

Cover design by Jim Sarfati
Reproduced with kind permission of the October Gallery, London. Taken from a painting by Gerald Wilde, "Intelligence Now", one of his recurrent themes, captures a new form: a brain-like shape with all the inner pathways revealed. Line curving, he breaks beyond Western logic and illustrates the practicality of non-linear thinking in the space and information age.

ISBN 1-891802-01-1

By The Way Books
P.O. Box 255869
Sacramento, CA 95865
916-482-2444 * FAX: 916-482-9898
www.bythewaybooks.com
Printed in Canada

This edition is dedicated to my dear friend
THE LATE EDWARD MATCHETT,
who died in Bristol, UK. December 1st 1998

Contents

Introduction

Manifesto

The Expressions

1. Intelligence communicates with intelligence 1
2. Making the meaningless meaningful 2
3. The need of intelligence 3
4. The need to progress 3
5. Communication with the future 4
6. Coalescence of vision and actuality 5
7. Fusion of meanings 6

8. Blocks to intelligence 6
9. Abandonment of what is not useful 7
10. Relation to material resources 9
11. Indifference to temporary states 10
12. Absence of anxiety 11
13. Involvement without involvement 11
14. The real goal 12

15. Maximization of meaning 13
16. Death and resurrection 14
17. Genesis 16
18. Self-renewing challenge 17
19. Quest and questioning 18
20. A new beginning now 21

21. Spontaneity 23

22. Changing the structure of now 24
23. Taking a real decision 25
24. Fusion of inner and outer 25
25. Being in control 26
26. God and egoism 27
27. The master of intelligence 28
28. Individuality 30
29. Right time, place, people, circumstances 31
30. A source of disturbance 35
31. Forms of emergence 35
32. The essence of evolution 37
33. Role of sacrifice 38
34. Higher and lower 39
35. Originality 40

36. Objectivity of purpose 41
37. Progress now 42
38. Acceleration 43
39. Reality of diversity 45
40. Control of complexity 46
41. Chaos and destruction 47
42. Non-violence 47

43. Specificity of sensitivities 48
44. Discrimination 49
45. Substantiality 50
46. Love and evil 51
47. Authentic wholeness 52
48. Heaven and earth 52
49. The unanswered question 53

CONTENTS

50. Media 53
51. The speaking part 55
52. Is mankind intelligent? 55
53. Concentration 56
54. Design 57
55. Perfection 58
56. Stupidity 58

Coda 59

Gerald Wilde & Intelligence Now 60
Edward Matchett 60
Anthony Blake 62

Twelve Hypotheses on Higher Intelligence 63

Introduction

The original title of this book was 'Intelligence Now'. Since it has been published now over twenty years, I think it now more fitting to simply call it 'Intelligence'.

The text arose out of a presentation given to a group of senior engineers at the Perkins Engine Company in Peterborough, UK, November 1972. The engineers were participating in an intense developmental exercise under the direction of Edward Matchett, an Englishman who pioneered radically new approaches to the development of creativity, genius and wisdom. This work required the creation and communication of a vision of intelligence that would "pull" upon the consciousness of those involved and open them to more profound levels of mental operation.

The talk was not an argued explanation, but like a hologram of expression. In the hologram, as opposed to the more usual photograph, every part of the film contains a record of the whole scene: a small bit of the hologram film can be used to produce the totality of the image. But the use of just one small bit produces a very fuzzy picture.

More than fifty expressions of the idea of intelligence were included in the talk, every one of them expressing the whole idea — but in its own unique way. The idea of intelligence was presented in a community of expressions, in which the inter-relevance of themes and examples was left unsaid. Because reading is a less lively occupation than listening, some of the gaps have been filled in for the production of this text. As with all abstractions, it is totally misleading when taken as a starting point for thinking, unless in the company of a large mass of ideas and observations belonging to personal experience.

A hypertext version of this book was produced in 1995 and made available on the Web as a "tuning-up device". The advent of hypertext made what I was groping for some years ago come more within reach. Inter-relevance appeared to be accessible in a new way. The hypertext medium can help to evoke 'the same' in ourselves. In every moment, creative and needed connections are being formed within the field of our information. Very likely, the world is 'written' in hypertext!

Because of the prompting of a small but articulate number of active readers, I was persuaded to produce a new 'hard-copy' version. Once we have the 'organizing idea' of hypertext, we can read an interconnected set of texts more easily on paper than on the computer screen.

This text would not have been possible without the work of: Edward Matchett relating to the ideas; Brian Turner, Bruno Martin and Richard Clemens relating to production; Theodore Shab and Jason Josslyn relating to hypertext; Gerald Wilde and Kathy Mitchell relating to non-verbal inspiration (unfortunately, we are not able to include the remarkable drawings made by Kathy in this edition). I am grateful to By the Way Books for their commitment and support in bringing about this new edition, which derives from much work on the part of the people mentioned that is no longer visible.

I must mention in particular the remarkable painting *Intelligence Now*, which is reproduced on the front cover, by one of the leading English abstract expressionists, Gerald Wilde. I served as the passive stimulus for this powerful work. A brief note on the artist and the painting appears at the end of the book.

The poem, which appears as the 'Manifesto' in this edition, was written by me in Prague in August 1968. By sheer chance, I took the last train out of the city before the Russians invaded. The inspiration for this book probably came from the Prague Spring; but, who knows the real origin of anything?

Since 1968, I have felt a cyclicity of events at work, proceeding at an ever-faster rate. This little book has continued to serve as a sign post through all the various 'shocks' and manifestations I and my friends have been subject to in the 'generation when the world did change'. Now, the signs are visible to all.

Thirty years on! The human condition is ever more perilous, yet there are signs of new influences. Intelligence is the most flexible aspect of the universe. I have come to take up the challenge put to us by John Bennett many years ago: to *communicate* with and also to *understand* 'higher intelligence'. It is now an integral part of the program of work of the *DuVersity*. The DuVersity is a response to the need for thinking and acting in accordance with 'diversity in unity' instead of fixed, single-valued and linear ways and, essentially, emerged from the thinking of this little book.

—Anthony Blake, *the Cotswolds 1998*

Manifesto

Reconstruction —
it takes a long time
but it is here, now.
Now there is a going forward,
the past is disowned,
becomes crude foundations.
The piles must go deep
searchingly into what is solid.
The construction —
it must not be weak,
liable to collapse
and recrimination.
It must make room enough
for the new people —
they will pass through a generation
when the world will change.

Anthony Blake, *Prague 1968*

The Expressions

Intelligence

I. Intelligence Communicates with intelligence

Intelligence communicates instantaneously with intelligence, wherever and in whatever it acts. This is so between people, between a musician and his instrument, between a person and an idea; even between an idea and an idea. We can understand the world because it has intelligence. The true scientist listens to the intelligence of Nature in a form of dialogue.

To perceive the intelligence of language, it is necessary to understand what language is saying; or, rather, that it *is*, essentially, saying. Intelligence is not confined to the brains of human beings. It is present in speech and present in our bodies; in the sky and all living things. The intelligence of something becomes present when intelligence touches it. So we, too, are awakened by the touch of intelligence: from an intelligent human, a poem, a landscape, an idea, or whatever. The moment of contact is mutual; there is no causality. Intelligence is in communication with intelligence.

Our human form of intelligence is not ultimate. There are oceans of intelligence in which we are only particles. But the intelligence in us can remember the oceans. Even the least thing has some degree of intelligence and belongs to the same oceans, which are unfathomable.

2. Making the meaningless meaningful

Intelligence transforms the meaningless into the meaningful. In the world of intelligence, **nothing is meaningless**: it is all transformable. For human beings, the confrontation with the meaningless is a powerful way of eliciting intelligence. Intelligence cannot stand what is meaningless. Unfortunately, we may be weak at withstanding the impact of the meaningless and settle for bundles of tiny meanings or meanings in separate compartments.

Intelligence does not close its eyes to any difficulty. Nothing is smoothed over. Rather, it leaps into a greater world, turning the force of contradiction into an element of the greater whole.

Ordinary criteria of positive and negative do not apply. The stress and noise of city life becomes transformed into an energy of meditation. Pain becomes a way of understanding the body. Moral suffering becomes a way of freedom from the personality. Mistakes become a way to truth. Lies become a way to sensitive perception. Death becomes a way to life. Anger becomes a way to compassion. The **inversion of the negative** is a major sign of intelligence.

nothing is meaningless

The mathematician Rudy Rucker gives a kind of 'proof' of an analogous proposition: that no number is un-interesting. He says: consider all the numbers one by one and find the last one that has any interesting properties; the number that comes next is then interesting just because it is the first one that is so!

inversion of the negative

The inversion of positive and negative requires a third force, neither positive nor negative, akin to both at once; but, in essence, a movement between the two.

"A typical human situation is that someone attacks you or insults you and you get upset. You want to deny reality to the criticism. You block out what it might mean. You just react. If

2

you just react, then you learn nothing from the encounter and at best you reach a stand-off. Action and reaction are equal and opposite, as Newton pointed out in physics centuries ago, and their net sum is a fat zero. If you want to gain something from the encounter, then you have to encompass the energy of your attacker and bring it inside yourself. This requires of you something that is independent of reaction, something that is impartial and aware.

"This 'something', this third force, gives you the possibility of going through the barriers of reaction that divide you from the attacker. You are able to 'be on his side' without losing your own side. You can bring out and express how you are hurt without becoming more weak. You can do this because you can take the initiative, and not simply react, or follow on from, the initiative of your attacker. It is, perhaps, this taking of the initiative that constitutes the crucial act in bringing about a change of fortune."

from *The Triad* by Anthony Blake

3. The need of intelligence

The world has to be remade every moment. Thus, every moment is an opportunity for making the world differently. Such is the way of intelligence.

If there is no new making, we are condemned to blind participation in the construction and maintenance of our own prisons.

Intelligence enables us to help the world and ourselves enter the unknown future. It is thread guiding us out of the labyrinth. It works by constantly redesigning the labyrinth so that we are never trapped.

4. The need to progress

Intelligence in man expresses itself in the need to progress. Evolution has provided man with a sense of this need, though in most people it is fragmented and not understood. When it awakens, there is no going back. Whatever the situation of an intelligent man, he must progress in that situation and make the situation progress. If he does not, he "dies" and has to be "reincarnated" again in another situation. Intelligence can only go forward.

5. Communication with the future

Intelligence is a connection with the pattern of the future. This pattern is both the nexus of trends acting from the past and an expression of the spirit that occasioned the evolution of life and man. It is a pattern of creative opportunities, woven together in the ocean of intelligence as liquid crystals, moving, dynamic, more than alive.

The future directs us to make sense of the past. Like salmon going up the river, we swim in the current of the future. The creative future appears in human life as unexpected impulses, dreams, visions, the sense of "something more". These are more than reactions to the past or accidents of the present. The future has a coherence of its own, far beyond our conceptions of order. The future commands without force, asks without coercion.

Mankind has one future and we belong to that one future. Look to history and evolution and see how the future pulls on the past. The creative future is on the other side of fear and smallness. We can realize that future. There is work to be done, holes in the fabric of the universe needing to be filled by creative action, intelligent human action.

Whatever the time-space situation of man, intelligence operates from and with what is beyond. What is beyond is a plenitude, not of actual things, but of things needed to be done and in ways not yet thought of.

6. Coalescence of vision and actuality

Intelligence combines vision and actuality with no compromise. Intelligence works through the unexpected. It makes the most extreme ideal a practical reality. It renders what is actual supremely meaningful by enabling it to realize the ideal. Jerusalem is already **in England's green and pleasant land**. People without intelligence often do not see Jerusalem at all.

The usual opposition of the ideal and actual is not resolved by a miraculous *fiat* but by the work of intelligence. People who stop at the opposition, stop this side of the door of intelligence. Intelligence begins with the impossible, not the probable or feasible.

in England's green and pleasant land

> And did those feet in ancient time
> > Walk upon England's mountains green?
> And was the holy Lamb of God
> > On England's pleasant pastures seen?

> And did the Countenance Divine
> > Shine forth upon our clouded hills?
> And was Jerusalem builded here
> > Among the dark Satanic Mills?

> Bring me my arrows of burning gold!
> > Bring me my arrows of desire!
> Bring me my spear! O clouds, unfold!
> > Bring me my chariot of fire!

> I will not cease from mental fight,
> > Nor shall the sword sleep in my hand,
> Till we have built Jerusalem
> > In England's green and pleasant land.
> > > from *Milton* by William Blake

7. Fusion of meanings

Intelligence is a quantum jump between meaning and meaning. That is why intelligence is often obscured from sight. It appears to come from what has been established. In reality, it is simply that intelligence is naturally connected with what is meaningful — past, present and future. It is not a cutting off of the past. It can be an enrichment of past events and at the same time, the start of something new.

We usually see only one side. After intelligence has operated in us, we mechanically reconstruct the event *backwards*. It seems that what has happened is even a logical consequence of the past. In reality, intelligence leapt out of a new point of meaning towards a familiar one. We see the new life in the familiar point of meaning (a piece of mathematics, a poem, an idea, a theory) and do not see the new point of meaning. That new point will continue to operate, but unconsciously. The unknown meaning has incarnated in the familiar one and we do not recognize it, save through a vague sense that "something is different". So we become discouraged and believe only in the familiar form and lose faith in the possibilities of "escape" or going further. We have already gone further. We need to remember more accurately.

8. Blocks to intelligence

There are blocks to intelligence in people. These are manifold and can be removed only through intelligence. Such things as *illusion* (false beliefs about the nature of the world and human nature; fantasies about creativity; upside-down ideas about the causes of events in human life), *self-doubting* (false humility; pessimism; "thinking little"; psychopathic mental masochism; bungling introspection; lack of positive ideals; cheapness of vision), *fear* (attachment to what is known; anxious rejection of the unknown; clinging to present understanding; no wish to take responsibility for oneself; avoidance of questioning and suffering; emptiness of self-creation); *ordinary desires and hungers* (rejection of "useless passions"; attachment to spurious goals of happiness; puerility of vision of possibilities; passive acceptance of the lower instead of the higher; useless restlessness; repetition of experiences; mechanicality and animality; lack of influence over inner energies), *self-satisfaction* (accepting achievement of the familiar as success; reducing the world to fit one's smallness; rewriting reality to make it fit self-image; comfortableness and homeostasis; avoidance of "shocks"; attachment to achievement, status and role), *herd instinct* (inability to think for oneself; passivity in the face of accidental circumstantial standards; identification with non-human characteristics; mutual slavery; pathetic fear of loneliness; mutual masturbation, stagnation, closure of thinking), *protectiveness* (escape from challenge; avoidance of disclosure; negativity towards real progress on the part of others; sentimentality instead of love; talking to oneself to make everything "seem all right"), *laziness* (not wanting to pay for achievement; superstitious belief in "manna"; reliance on others; lack of persistence; substituting images for action).

9. Abandonment of what is not useful

Intelligence abandons anything that is not useful: it is as if the useless element ceases to exist. The useless element may be a whole social system, in which case energy and interest is attracted away from it, leaving just a shell that gradually disintegrates and disappears. Such a dissolution may appear a painful process to those attached to the institution and they may fight like fury to preserve the status of what possesses them and even destroy the body of intelligence bringing change. So, in our own minds, the useless element will grow fearful and furious at impending death, or strive to attract attention to itself.

Intelligence in itself has no mercy. Mercy comes from something higher still and can be inspired by a love that seeks to embrace all things — even to the outer darkness of insignificance. That is not the role of intelligence, which must progress. In human history, most happenings drop below the critical level of significance and disappear in entropy.

The dreams of grandeur of **Ozymandias** reduce to unknown ruins in the sand. The inevitable struggles and sufferings of countless billions of people perish with them. **Ivan Osokin** stares at the street and realises that his death or life has no significance in the course of events.

What decides significance is not the mechanics of wars, politics, economics, geography and the like but intelligence. Where intelligence has worked is a living presence that lives outside of ordinary time. We must be prepared for the loss of favourite attitudes and approaches.

Ozymandias

> I met a traveller from an antique land
> Who said: Two vast and trunkless legs of stone
> Stand in the desert . . . Near them, on the sand,
> Half shrunk, a shattered visage lies, whose frown,
> And wrinkled lip, and sneer of cold command,
> Tell that its sculptor well those passions read
> Which yet survive, stamped on these lifeless things,
> The hand that mocked them, and the heart that fed:
> And on the pedestal these words appear:
> 'My name is Ozymandias, king of kings:
> Look on my works, ye Mighty, and despair.'
> Nothing beside remains. Round the decay
> Of that colossal wreck, boundless and bare
> The lone and level sands stretch far away.
>
> *Ozymandias* by Percy Shelley (1792-1822)

Ivan Osokin

> "Osokin looks around, and suddenly an extraordinarily vivid sensation sweeps over him that, if he were not there, everything would be exactly the same."
>
> from *The Strange Life of Ivan Osokin* by P. D. Ouspensky

10. Relation to material resources

Intelligence is not restricted by any limitations on resources: materials, people, money, knowledge, etc. It can always achieve something, no matter how little is available. Evidence abounds for this and for its corollary: abundance of resources is no guarantee of intelligence. An intelligent being can make a time-machine with string and a safety pin. This does not mean that anything can be done 'at will'. Intelligence is in harmony with the laws and patterns of the universe and life. It respects the **denying force**. It is simply that reality is far more flexible than, for example, our thinking. Also, intelligence is not a matter of solving already defined problems, because it creates its own goals according to the emergent situation in which it participates.

denying force

> "One of the most profound and unexpected teachings implicated in Gurdjieff's logic of threefoldness is that what may appear to us as negative and the thwarting of our good intentions is deeply connected with our freedom, and is a *holy force* just as affirmation is. The denying force is the only way we can enter the evolutionary flux. It is just when there is resistance, recalcitrance, revolt that we can make a *new beginning*. Whenever we start from confidence and positive energy, we are bound to go downhill from then on."
>
> from *The Triad* by Anthony Blake

II. Indifference to temporary states

Intelligence is completely indifferent to temporary suffering and happiness. These are zero in its equation. Thus, it often happens that the operations of intelligence appear to be cold-blooded and lacking in concern. It is only later that their truly human worth becomes apparent. In developing intelligence, it is essential to overcome attachment to ephemeral satisfactions and mechanical avoidance of pain or difficulty. And this is to be achieved not by effort or will power, but by treating them as zero in the equation of intelligence itself. Happiness and suffering remain — but their significance changes. It is especially important for a man to sacrifice his attachment to his **suffering**. Suffering is an inevitable factor in existing and being alive; and the failure to understand suffering is one of the major signs of the lack of intelligence in our world today.

suffering

> "Another thing people must sacrifice is their suffering. It is very difficult to sacrifice ones suffering. A man will renounce any pleasures you like but he will not give up his suffering. Man is made in such a way that he is never so much attached to anything as he is his suffering. And it is necessary to be free from suffering. No one is not free from suffering, who has not sacrificed his suffering, can work . . . Nothing can be attained without suffering but at the same time one must begin by sacrificing suffering. Now decipher what this means."

from *In Search of the Miraculous* by P. D. Ouspensky

12. Absence of anxiety

Intelligence cannot operate where there is anxiety. Anxiety is slavery to the fear of not knowing. Intelligence knows and does not know equally. Intelligence is freedom from anxiety. This is not to say that stress, a sense of urgency, the burden of complex demands, in any way are barriers to intelligence, although they are frequently causes of anxiety. The stress can be there without anxiety; and it may be an essential part of the challenge which awakens intelligence.

The traditional association of intelligence with leisure is significant. There is nothing in intelligence itself which is hurried, stressful or tense. Intelligence operates in its own time — so it has all the time in the world.

Intelligence is patient in front of the inevitable working out of events. It does not attach itself to immediate action, but directs appropriate action, which may entail a wait of a thousand days or the planting of a seed that will take centuries to come to fruition. But what appears as a virtue — patience — is in reality a perception of the working of things on a time scale outside of the ordinary.

13. Involvement without involvement

Intelligence is not a specific kind of action. It may consist in doing nothing when all the tendencies are to do. It may be in silence or in protest. It may involve moving heaven and earth, or sitting still. Intelligence changes the course of events without being an event itself. It does not enter into causal chains, it is not in the realm of action and reaction, so what is intelligent is usually unperceived or confused with something else. In this sense, intelligence is something totally unknowable by the mind, which concerns itself with the appearance of events.

14. The real goal

Intelligence does not obey external criteria of consistency. It can produce actions that appear to be unconnected or contradictory — because it operates in terms of the particularities of each moment. It uses the material of the moment itself and does not carry a standard "bag of tricks" with it along its way. A total action of intelligence may compose a multitude of operations, the significance of any one of which cannot be "read" in isolation from the others.

Intelligence is in what is done and achieved. It does not complete its manifestation in what is displayed, whether in thought or on paper. This shows in the difference between a mathematical demonstration and a mathematical proof. The former can be operated by a computer and consists in explicit operations of the substitution of signs according to definite rules. The proof is something different. What is said in the proof evokes the intelligence to realize it.

Intelligence is well able to explain its conduct in terms of logic, scientific method and scholarship, but it is impatient with the low standards and limited horizons of such things. It will turn logic to its own purposes! All existing systems of thinking and behavior become merely instruments in the hands of intelligence and not ends. Intelligence sees that what is appropriate at one moment is inappropriate at another and acts accordingly. The external explanation that appears to work for the first moment fails for the second; and this failure of explanation is turned into a criticism of the phenomena, and the intelligence is called "inconsistent", "illogical", "random", etc.

For a musician, what has to be done is making music — not producing thoughts about the making of music. It is a common characteristic of the mind that it confuses primary and secondary activities. Seeing what needs to be done, and in what this doing consists, is of the nature of intelligence.

15. Maximization of meaning

In essence, intelligence is concerned with maximizing meaning in every situation in which it operates. The possibilities open to intelligence at any moment are vast: it is in tune with the inner dynamism of the universe and of history. Intelligence can gather threads of creative potential into a fusion with available resources and circumstances. Thus, it creates, or realizes, meaning. It is this facility of access to the dynamism of the universe and absence of illusion concerning the material state of affairs that enables intelligence to be an agent of progress, moving from concentration to concentration of meaning, enlarging and deepening what is truly significant.

The intelligent man, locked in solitary confinement, can bring about a concentration of meaning in the form of games with a friendly spider. However isolated an operation of intelligence appears, it will be an essential part of the whole pattern of intelligence. Eventually, the spider is trained to send messages.

The material state of affairs constrains what is material, or things. Intelligence does not deal with things, but meanings. The universe of meaning is the primary ecology.

16. Death and resurrection

Intelligence is allied to death and resurrection. For intelligence to come, the old must go. Do we put **new wine in old bottles**? In particular, the mind must give way. This is known in a half-baked fashion by many people. They recognize that when the mind is fatigued and relinquishes its hold, new insights can come. They recognize the spark there is in madness, ecstasy, dreams, and the visions provided by hallucinogenic drugs. What is not widely known is that the mind can be deliberately made to "die" — by withdrawing the animating spirit from it. The quiet state is a death of the mind; perhaps very close to sleep, but it must be a dreamless sleep, as if near to death. In the quiet, the intelligence can resurrect the mind into an inner vision: there is a "resurrection body" within the mind.

The death of the mind can be painful in that it involves the relinquishment of its passions and habits and usual activities and movements, all of which strive to carry on, all of which continue to cry "I". As one watches the mind, the will of the watcher is trapped in the content of the mind, which takes control. This happens when one wants to remain a mental entity, and not to "die". Yet, if the mind dies, a new world appears — in a strange clarity. For all this to happen properly, however, it is necessary to, as Gurdjieff put it, "**consciencely descend**". Each step must be watched and tested in the heart. When the darkness is reached, the watching must still go on.

In solving a complex problem, maybe it is that one's manner of thinking must die, or an attitude die, or a particular criterion which overrides everything give way. Something has to die. Here is a particular fashion of sacrifice: thus, the death must be for real, really felt, consciously observed, but not thought of as something which one does. Death is not at our command. We have to submit to death. There is no concern here with suicide! So, in the dying of a meditator, he may call on God to guide and comfort him into another world. And the power of God will cause his resurrection in a glorious new body — to think and act once more, but with a larger vision.

In a more ordinary sense, intelligence cannot operate unless what the person has achieved so far has died for him. He or she must be free to begin completely anew. This is resurrection.

new wine in old bottles
> "There is some substance that is different from experience, and this substance we are going to call 'wisdom'. It is a substance if we say it can be taken from some source and poured into people, or enter people to fill something in them - something that corresponds to a bottle or vessel . . .
> "Even when some of the wine of Wisdom enters, because there is already a soured false imagination, it also becomes soured. Although we can have Wisdom, it quickly becomes sour in us."
>
> from *Sacred Influences* by John Bennett

consciencely descend
> In Gurdjieff's *Toast of the Idiots* (see *Gurdjieff: anatomy of a myth* by James Moore for an outline description of the ritual) if a man or woman reach the condition of 'Enlightened Idiot' then nothing can help them, and their only recourse is to 'consciencely descend' back down to being ordinary idiot and start all over again.

17. Genesis

Intelligence has no termination, it is always a beginning, a changing, an advancing. This is so because it is associated with creative futures, not elements of the past. This provides a valuable test for intelligence, and a test for intelligence that can invoke intelligence. Intelligence is utterly naive and has no idea that there already exist "proven ways" of doing things. What people call their 'understanding' is too slow and heavy to be of any help. Intelligence begins to begin, always, helpless and childlike.

Thus, intelligence is joyful. "**New every morning** is the love my waking and arising prove", as the old hymn says. There is no boredom (though there will be labour). Every act of intelligence makes a new man, even though the man may not know this himself.

new every morning
"New every morning is the love
our awakening and uprising prove;
through sleep and darkness safely brought,
restored to life and power and thought.

New mercies, each returning day,
hover around us while we pray;
new perils past, new sins forgiven,
new thoughts of God, new hopes of heaven.

If on our daily course our mind
be set to hallow all we find,
new treasures still, of countless price,
God will provide for sacrifice.

The trivial round, the common task,
will furnish all we need to ask,
room to deny ourselves, a road
to bring us daily nearer God.

Only, O Lord, in thy dear love
fit us for perfect rest above;
and help us, this and every day,
to live more nearly as we pray."
    Hymns Ancient and Modern, no. 2 by John Keble (1792-1864)

18. Self Renewing Challenge

Intelligence creates self-challenge. Most people recognize the need of challenge to produce awakening, especially: danger, intensity of demand, complexity, contradiction, a cry for help. Usually, such challenges act upon us by circumstances outside of us, over which we have no control. What we can control is no challenge!

The greatest self-challenge is contained in a sense of need, a sense that has become a distinct call to intelligence. Then, a man is no longer dependent on the accidents of circumstance to bring about the inner reorientation requisite to the operation of his intelligence. The real challenge is one in which all that a man is left with is the facility to call on his intelligence. Thoughts, formulae, beliefs, postures, assumptions, world view — all are found lacking. Nothing will do but intelligence.

With intelligence, however, the self-renewing challenge is incorporated in its very essence. As one is lifted up to new heights, greater ones loom over the horizon. Intelligence cannot rest easy or satisfied. Its prompting will create danger and surprise, will put people in touch with the unexpected. And intelligence working in a man will wake him up to defects, false beliefs and possibilities of new achievements that, in their turn, call up intelligence to do its work.

To get into that condition deliberately requires intelligence. It is the gold of the alchemists, which requires gold to begin with. It is like the consciousness which is needed to make ourselves more conscious, or the **knowledge we need to collect** in order to understand. Intelligence comes only from intelligence.

knowledge we need to collect

> "The fact is that the enormous majority of people do not want any knowledge whatever; they refuse their share of it and do not even take the ration allotted to them, in the general distribution, for the purposes of life. . . Owing to this, enormous quantities of knowledge remain, so to speak, unclaimed and can be distributed amongst those who realise its value."
>
> from *In Search of the Miraculous* by P. D. Ouspensky

19. Quest and questioning

Intelligence is a questing thing. It is difficult to say whether intelligence leads to the quest or the quest to intelligence. Every time a man poses a question that opens his heart and mind, he calls to intelligence. Yet it is intelligence that enables him to pose the question.

There are no substantial questions that come from the habitual mind, which is full of answers. There are no adequate causal reasons for the arising of a real question. A real question connects with noticing and decision or commitment. Thus, a man **notices some anomaly** in his own behavior or in a theory; he asks, "Why is this? What does this mean?"; he commits himself to an investigation to elucidate the answers. Such a picture is a picture of an intelligent being, **not of the habitual mind**, which reduces anomalies to fit some convenient category of explanation.

For the awakening of intelligence, **Shivapuri Baba** advised people to question constantly. Such questionings are a quest for reality that act as invocations to one's inner intelligence. However, they must be real questions, asked by the whole of the man, not merely a string of words in the mind.

If we ask, the answer will come. If we reject all lesser things, an answer of value will come — though maybe in a form that is not expected.

Real questioning requires strong determination, discrimination and patience. If we could align ourselves with a real question for one hour, extraordinary changes would result. As it is, the ordinary man asks a question in a momentary spasm. He may not even notice that he is no longer asking the question, or that it has become simply a cyclic eddy current in his associations. The gain and loss of reality in questioning needs to be carefully watched with the patience to again and again begin again and renew the act of opening and questing that offers a beginning of intelligence. All real questions issue from the primal quest of a potentially intelligent individual: "Why do things not make sense?" "What is the reality?" "Who am I?"

notices some anomaly

"Likewise, an all-round awareness of everything concerning these sacred laws also conduces, in general, to this, that three-brained beings irrespective of the form of their exterior coating, by becoming capable in the presence of all cosmic factors not depending on them and arising round about them - both the personally favourable as well as the unfavourable - of pondering on the sense of existence, acquire data for the elucidation and reconciliation in themselves of that, what is called, 'individual collision' which often arises, in general, in three-brained beings from the contradiction between the concrete results flowing from the processes of all the cosmic laws and the results presupposed and even quite surely expected by their what is called 'sane-logic'; and thus, correctly evaluating the essential significance of their own presence, they become capable of becoming aware of the genuine corresponding place for themselves in these common-cosmic actualizations."

from *All and Everything* by G. I. Gurdjieff

not of the habitual mind

". . . I think that antiquity had very good reason to enumerate the first inventors of the noble arts among the gods, seeing that the common intellects have so little curiosity . . . The application to great invention moved by small hints and the thinking, that under a primary and childish appearance admirable arts may be hidden, is not the part of a trivial but a superhuman spirit"

from *The Starry Messenger* by Galileo (1564-1642)

Shivapuri Baba

The Shivapuri Baba (also called Sri Govindananda Bharati) lived from 1826 to 1963. During his life, he spent 40 years walking round the world. He taught an uncompromising three-fold discipline: spiritual, moral and physical.

". . . as a result of our inquiry into the inner depths of our earthly existence, we find that our body is not ourselves. The finer principles beyond this body-consciousness which we call soul is our real self. This soul is to be known and realized for better identification. . . . This inquiry as to 'Who am I?' should be our main concern."

"'Who am I?' is our question. 'O God, reveal to me the secret'. Thus praying we go on with an agitated mind and spend all the rest of our time. . . . we must go on with our original question as to 'Who am I?'. As long as this Truth of truths is not revealed to us we must not stop our agitation or else we are doomed."

from *Long Pilgrimage* (the life and teachings of the Shivapuri Baba) by John Bennett.

20. A new beginning now

Everything in which we are involved — events, thoughts, interactions with other people and so on — has already begun. That is to say, what is happening has already been set in motion. We find ourselves in the midst of things going on. Every act of intelligence transforms this going on of things so that some new element enters. For this to be truly so and not simply a superficial addition to the stream of events, intelligence must be capable of creating new beginnings. Such new beginnings are outside of the causal nexus — that is, of one event leading to another within an established framework of conditions.

A possibility for us is a present moment which is whole, in which every part and every aspect expresses the same unique character that, in itself, is invisible and formless. This view of the present moment differs greatly from that in which it appears as a cross section of a bundle of temporal events. The present moment that has wholeness is substantial and in the operations of intelligence, this substance is restructured in a way neither timeless nor temporal. What is now is unmade and recreated while remaining now.

On a lower level, this affords a test of intelligence which differentiates it quite unmistakably from problem-solving and the like. Intelligence creates the problem while evolving a solution, whereas problem-solving computes within the conditions set. So, too, intelligence gets around the constraints of space and time.

It does this, not by abolishing these constraints (which it cannot do) but by bringing into manifestation something of the **unconditioned**. Put in other terms, intelligence is the bridge between quality and quantity.

When the unconditioned enters the conditioned, a new kind of experience emerges, free of the mechanical stream of events, yet intimately involved with them. Such emergences are sometimes called "insights", and it is true that the significant change that takes place is in seeing. But the person does not "have" the insight. The person must give way, recognize all of himself as conditioned here

21

and now and in total, and allow what is not conditioned to enter.

The unconditioned is invisible and whole. It enters by way of holes in the visible. When one sees that the totality of what is visible is inadequate, that there is a lack not to be made good by anything that is visible or any amount of it, then it is possible to relinquish the power of the visible and ask of the invisible its healing touch.

The unconditioned finds its own way. One is not in a position to be its guide or mentor. One plays the role of witness of things as they are, and does not presume to know in the same way how things can be. The unconditioned finds its way into the most complex and detailed parts, without effort and not through a process. It is in its very nature to do this.

Unconditioned

The idea of the Unconditioned appears in all traditions which allow for many worlds. The Unconditioned is free to enter into any world and is not simply a transcendental abstraction. Contrasted with the conditioned, it appears in Hinduism as arupa (formless) in contrast with rupa (form). In the 'Teachings of Don Juan', it appears as the nagual in contrast with the tonal. In systems which allow for a gradation of worlds, such as the Sufi one of four worlds; it is lahut (the boundless, the unfathomable) in contrast with the three relative worlds pertaining to 'possibilities', 'spirits' and 'bodies'.

"One Sufi teacher described it like this: 'This lahut offers its breasts for whoever is able to drink it to relieve its own overflowing nothingness.' "

"He [Rumi] says: 'If you want to enter into that place, leave your existence behind. If you want to find the worker, go into the workshop; the workshop is nothingness."

from *Deeper Man* by John Bennett

21. Spontaneity

Intelligence is not a matter of premeditation in the sense of planning. Thinking, acting and willing become one whole: there is not thought and then action; not a weighing of alternatives and the making of a choice; no separation of the person from his action. Thus, intelligence operates by way of emergence. Out of an involvement in a situation, a new line of intentionality emerges. The new line may at first be unrecognized and there is need of discipline, attention and sensitivity to allow what is intelligent to gain a place and produce the appropriate development.

The idea of an intentionality that is not thought out or associated with a mental picture may appear strange, but it is essential to an understanding of intelligence. In the first stages of intelligent emergence, the new intention may be noticed more as a mood, a shift of concern, a concentration of wishing, a shift in the objects of desire, and so on; rather than anything directly to do with achieving results or getting into action. Intelligence affects the whole man, but initially finds expression in those aspects of him that are most free and able to change. Hence the association of intelligence with the nonconscious, with reverie and dream, with hallucination and emotional excitement, sexual activity and religious feeling. Often enough, intelligence calls to a man from some part of him that his habitual mind has learned to scorn; and since the gateway of all transformation of energy and realization of meaning is the present there is not room for both such a mind and the emergence of something new.

22. Changing the structure of now

The beginning begins when **the present** is made different. The restructuring of now is not a fashioning in time, but a gathering of the meaningful parts in the calling of intelligence. There is no movement, but communication within the present moment becomes real.

There are whole disciplines of intelligence concerned entirely with enabling people to come to the point at which they can recognize and align themselves with the signals of intelligence. These disciplines often appear to have nothing to do with making progress or achieving results, but they require strong intelligence to make them effective.

the present

"The Present Moment is the field of operation of a will. The present moment is a state of incessant flux under influences entering from sources that we call 'past', 'future', 'form', 'pattern', 'decision', 'freedom'. "

from *The Dramatic Universe, Vol. IV* by John Bennett.

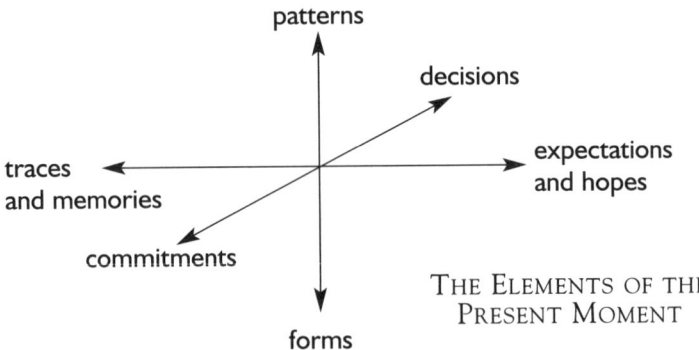

THE ELEMENTS OF THE
PRESENT MOMENT

23. Taking a real decision

When intelligence operates, it becomes possible for a man to take real decisions, committing his body and mind in obedience to a demanding task. Such tasks may appear to have an unnecessary level of demand in them, in that they are associated with the highest standards and aims conceivable. It is perhaps this side of intelligence that is most frightening to people, for it reveals unmistakably that the highest things are a real possibility for a man and thereby puts into question the worth of all ordinary strivings and intentions (which are so often a dedication to the status quo).

24. Fusion of inner and outer

Intelligence is a fusion of the inner and outer by something that is neither. "Inner" and "outer" are important realities for any being, without which it could not be a being. However, the distinction of inner and outer is not a fixed and is not made by a material boundary. It is totally dependent on the manner of willing.

For **Michelangelo**, was the chisel, the hammer, the marble, the idea in the marble, his arms ... outside? In creative work, the boundary of inner and outer changes, dissolves, is reformed. The 'I' that believes "I think" is, for example, a product of Indo-European grammar, socially indoctrinated from outside. With progress in meditation, one begins to see that one's mind is outside and one's thoughts are as personal as the clouds in the sky.

In the operations of intelligence, 'I' can go anywhere and be anything. But that is when the mind is left alone to run itself.

Michelangelo
"The marble not yet carved can hold the form
  Of every thought the greatest artist has,
  And no conception can yet come to pass
  Unless the hand obeys the intellect."
                    from *Sonnets (no. XV)* by Michelangelo
                    (translated by Elizabeth Jennings)

25. Being in control

In outward appearances, too, intelligence in operation seems to make the individual act in a way outside of "his control". He will not be able or willing to find reasons for what he does; he will change direction in inexplicable ways; he will not be able to antic-ipate what he is going to do, or how. But he will be set on a line or arrow of intention and will refuse to give up this line, even though he does not appear to "know what he is doing". With intelligence in operation, **ordinary notions of self-control and self-direction** are hopelessly inadequate. There is no need for "conscious steering" according to charts already prepared: the way of the voyage is into uncharted regions and all navigational aids will have to be devel-oped in the course of the journey, as they are needed. Thus, where-as we ordinarily conceive of control as: having a picture of where we are going, seeing where we are actually moving and applying cor-rections to maintain a direction: intelligent control requires no pic-ture — even of semi-determined destinations — and no long-wind-ed techniques of measurement and correction, for intelligence is already at the destination, as well as in the vehicle of the journey, and an inner communication leads to a coalescence that is mea-sured in meaning.

All this is possible because intelligence is not reducible to oper-ations with actuality alone, but is at home with many different lev-els and qualities of existence, including perhaps **non-actual states of matter,** as real as what is actual but ordinarily un-perceived.

ordinary notions of self-control and self-direction
"Now, we're suggesting that thought is a system belonging to the whole culture and society, evolving over history, and it creates the image of an individual who is supposed to be the source of thought."

from *Thought as a System* by David Bohm

non-actual states of matter

"VIRTUALITY: The state of hyle [matter] in which existence is wholly potential. Virtuality is relative so that any ratio of potential to actual is possible."

"VIRTUE: The measure of the potentiality of an entity or system for diversity of actualisation."

from *The Dramatic Universe, Vol. I* by John Bennett

26. God and egoism

Intelligence is controlled by what is God in us. This may be the spirit of our true selves: the "I" that is truly whole, not a fragmentary pattern of thinking or feeling, nor one of the many personalities that haunt our bodies. This "I" is the core of all our real decisions; and its command, once accepted in our being, must be obeyed utterly. For many people, the only real decision the "I" has made is to be born.

Only "I" can control intelligence. "I" can allow itself to act as a particle of Love or Truth. "I" is truly capable of what we call "Faith". "I" is the pure will in us, not in need of instruments or awareness to belong to reality. "I" is our God.

Yet, intelligence can be controlled by egoism: the will that claims reality for itself, not itself for reality. This is the "evil will", whose reality men can never bring themselves to face because it seems utterly beyond all possible reason. The evidence of destructive and evil intelligence is overwhelming. The proper struggle for individuality has often become an occasion for dreadful acts. People wake up to the paucity of meaning and the absurdity of ordinary values and beliefs and find release in bending the world to their own purposes. The evil that is done is projected into the same world that then deserves to suffer! That falsity leads eventually to self-destruction unless help is given and accepted (as Margaret gave to Faust). In the stream of difficult but ordinary tasks, the "God-criterion" is supremely important. For "I" to control intelligence, self-interest needs to be sacrificed. For egotism to exercise control, self-interest needs to be made the centre of value.

Since most people, even the most intelligent, represent a mixture of the egotistical and the divine, there is a real need always to ask: "What is God for me? Is what I am doing of use to the Whole?" To learn to ask these questions intelligently may take a long time, but they are of overwhelming importance for the individual and his capacity for intelligent operation.

27. The master of intelligence

It is difficult, but necessary for a right understanding, to realize that intelligence is not confined to the functioning of the human cerebral cortex. Intelligence is at work in the evolution of life and the solar system and the galaxy. In a sense, it is "**in the very air** we breathe". Exposure to the full extent and depth of intelligence would probably destroy us. It is far nearer the truth to assume that our "intelligent behavior" is but a minor manifestation of a universal intelligence than that this behavior is the very acme of the intelligence of the universe. We share in the workings of intelligence with all life on the earth. In this sense, we are no more in control of the workings of intelligence than animals are.

However, there is a difference between our situation and that of the animals: we have access to an intelligence that is truly our own if we choose to live in accordance with its laws. This intelligence is the agent of our individual uniqueness, that is, of the will that can operate through what we are. It is this that makes possible what is evil.

By taking risks and living outside of ordinary conventions, the creative intelligence, which is within the workings of our mind, can certainly be released. But there is no guarantee in all of this that the end result will not make us apart from the whole - which encompasses our fellow men and fellow creatures and the spiritual unity of the cosmos. The master of intelligence can be egoism. In the short term, the workings of an egoistic intelligence can have tremendous impact, but in the long term, the rejection of universal intelligence — within which all are equal — leads to a terrifying isolation.

The universal and the individual intelligence are not two separate things, but two modes, in which freedom can operate in a conditioned world. The particular and the universal are twin manifestations of a holistic spirit.

The master of intelligence is what is free. This begins in freedom from itself.

in the very air
   "The Teaching is like air.
   "Man dwells in it, but cannot realise by real feeling that but for it he would be dead.
   "He can see air only when it is polluted, as in smoke rising, and by its effects.
   . . . He may become aware of it, and profit more from it, by realising that it is a common substance treated with such heedlessness that nobody observes its presence."
                     'Words of Israil of Bokhara' from *Thinkers of the East*
                                             by Idries Shah

28. Individuality

The operations of intelligence in a man must be an expression of who he is. Another way of putting this is to say that a man is an Idea, a higher Thought, and that all his actions and thoughts and states are manifestations, however distorted, mutually conflicting and ambiguous, of this Idea or Thought.

A man is not his mind, even though he might identify himself with his mind until the point of death and even beyond. One remembers the English philosopher Broad reporting contact with a colleague "in the beyond", who was still discussing problems of epistemology and quite unaware he was dead!

The difference between the operations of mind and those of intelligence are so marked in this domain that they constitute an excellent test to aid our discrimination. The intelligent act expresses the Whole of us. The mental act can express a computation of data only.

When intelligence awakens in a man, *who he is* is called into question, for himself and for others. This is especially remarkable when the man has been overwhelmed in his mind by the impact of *intelligence* and may be experiencing a sense of loss and a condition of emptiness and unknowing.

The question of who? is vastly different from questions of what? or how? It is possible to see the difference only with intelligence; there is nothing else by which to see the nature of the difference.

There comes about a peculiar inversion of ordinary thinking: instead of living in a world where "I think", "I act", the world is such that "The who I am thinks", "The who I am acts".

29. Right time, place, people, circumstances

Intelligence is not confined to brains and the degree of individuality we associate with distinct bodies and memories. It can operate
through groups of people in a given period of time. In Greek, there
is a word 'kairos' to designate the propitious time in which acts of
significance are possible. If appropriate combinations of people were
provided, operations of intelligence would manifest and important
steps of progress could be made. Not all times were equally "ripe" for
intelligence. Another tradition suggests that by gathering together
certain combinations of people, intelligence could be invoked
amongst them.

In our time, we will think of **Göttingen** in the 20's or the
Bauhaus in the 30's as centers of operations of intelligence. There
are, however, many other examples not in the visible spheres of art
or science and many examples of groupings which have failed or
produced spurious secondary results.

In Sufi traditions, it is axiomatic that the operations of intelligence require appropriate time, place, people and circumstances. It
is also claimed that there is "something" in all people which enables
them to instinctively sense what is "appropriate". Part of this sense
manifests itself in the fascination nearly all people have for coincidence. Thinkers such as Jung and Bennett have attempted to deal
with this realm — of **synchronicity** — on an equal footing with the
causal nexus of the natural sciences. The problem remains that in
the synchronous, there is always some element of uniqueness, and it
is just that uniqueness which makes the event significant.

Coincidence is the first sign of an inner resonance between out-
wardly unconnected things. What appears as "mere coincidence"
may be the veil covering a hidden intention of intelligence.
Individuals bring into effect coincidence in their own lives but
often fail to see the workings of intelligence in what happens. It may
appear strange to speak of intelligence operating without being consciously recognized by the man through whom the intelligence is
working; but the puzzlement derives largely from a lack of apprecia-

tion of the fragmented and disconnected condition of the ordinary man. Further, if there was not some intelligence working in our lives, we would quickly die or go mad. Often, our attachment to unfounded beliefs and our distorted apparatus of judgment are just what enable the intelligence to operate without interference from "good intentions" and the "will to control"!

The effects of heeded intelligence, when combined together in **right time, place, people and circumstances,** can produce an awakening that is in keeping with the true welfare of those involved and their environment. With the same "inner sense", the people involved will know what kind of sacrifice they are called upon to make; and that sense needs to be awakened.

Awakening of intelligence in groups is always accompanied by a special vividness in the sense of time, place and circumstances. Further, the individuals who participate in the event acquire a vividness of individuality that enables them to make special and unique contributions to the whole, contributions which appear to be linked together by some "inner necessity".

In this realm, however, there is need to put aside any association of intelligence with ordinary ideas of "thinking" and "having ideas". There is also need to relegate to insignificance ordinary differentiations in terms of status, level or importance of people and their activities. The "leader" becomes **administrative servant,** or clown, the "lackey" becomes the source of inspiration. Roles are reversed and turned upside down — not by exchange of labels but in terms of the living dynamism of the event.

Göttingen

"A highlight in every week of the term was the 'Study Group on Matter' conducted in Room 204 of the Institute by Born, Franck and Hilbert, gratis et privatissime. It became almost a tradition in the course of time for Hilbert to open the proceedings with a pretence of innocence in the question: 'Well now, gentlemen, I'd just like ye to tell me, what exactly is an atom?"

from *Brighter than a Thousand Suns* by Robert Jungk

Bauhaus

The Bauhaus was a great school of art that flourished in Germany between 1919 and 1933 (when it was closed by the National Socialists). Between 1919 and 1928, it was directed by Walter Gropius and included Kandinsky and Klee amongst its staff. It has tremendous influence on all the arts of the twentieth century, especially architecture and design.

"The vast cosmological vision evolved in Klee's theory does not supply the key to the symbolic or semantic interpretation of the images and signs which appear in his paintings; it rather explains how each one of those images, each of those signs, contains a truth which each man will read according to his own experience and will find a place for in the rhythm of his own existence, and yet retains the same value of truth for everyone. . . The association with everyday life, the possibility of the work of art existing on a practical plane; this is another theme which links Klee's poetics with the Bauhaus didactics."

from the *Preface* by Giulio Carlo Argan in *Notebooks: Vol. 1, The Thinking Eye* by Paul Klee

synchronicity

Synchronicity refers to a connectivity of meaning rather than cause and effect. Carl Jung worked with the physicist Wolfgang Pauli on the concept of synchronicity as complementary to causality. They proposed this diagram:

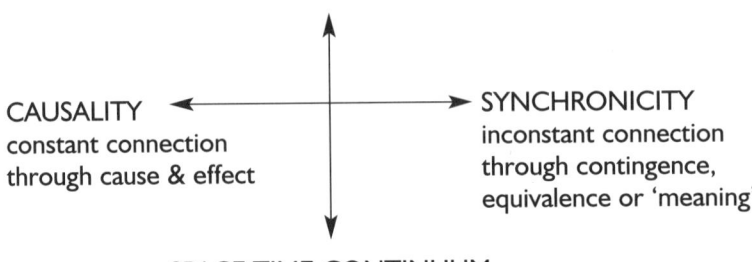

INDESTRUCTIBLE ENERGY

CAUSALITY
constant connection
through cause & effect

SYNCHRONICITY
inconstant connection
through contingence,
equivalence or 'meaning'

SPACE-TIME CONTINUUM

John Bennett in *The Dramatic Universe Vol. II* discusses the 'laws of synchronicity' in terms of the relationships between two 'hidden' kinds of 'time' - eternity and hyparxis - and space. John Allen calls these the 'laws of magic'.

time, place, people and circumstances
"The clash between the Sufis and the ordinary scholastic is strongly manifested in the theory that Sufi ideas can only be studied in accordance with certain principles: and these include time, place and people."

from 'The Time, the Place and the People' in *Tales of the Dervishes* by Idries Shah

administrative servant
In Herman Hesse's allegorical novel *The Journey to the East* the League of Searchers is assisted by the servant Leo. At the end of the novel, his true nature and status is revealed:
"His walk was light and peaceful, his robe sparkled with gold. He came nearer amid the silence of the assembly, and I recognised his walk, I recognised his movements, and finally recognised his face. It was Leo. In a magnificent, festive robe, he climbed through the rows of officials to the High Throne like a Pope. . . . I was no less deeply moved and amazed that it was Leo, the former porter and servant, who now stood at the head of the whole League and was ready to pass judgement on me."

30. A source of disturbance

The operations of intelligence have at their center what is unexpected. To the outside observer, what happens may appear as disturbing or even frightening. Those whose actions are evoked from intelligence often appear enigmatic, irrational, bizarre or as subject to a strange compulsion. Intelligence means the breaking-through of the unknown and changes in the reality of the known.

Intelligence has "no reason" for those to whom the need that it answers is invisible. It can inspire fear; but it can also so challenge cherished assumptions that those who are willing to suffer the process of change can be awakened. Indeed, every conscious acceptance of the "unthinkable" is a contribution to the development of intelligence. Those who train in this way can learn how to use other people as an almost constant source of disturbing factors; for other people are *incredible*.

31. Forms of Emergence

Intelligence is multifarious in its manifestations: it can operate through a movement of creative explosion, or through a quiet, almost unnoticed build-up of potential for the future. There are many other modes of manifestations, but the latter is singularly significant because the most neglected. Often enough, while the majority are concerned with lack of progress or change and keep themselves in a state of constant agitation and futile efforts, the man of intelligence will remain unmoved, being aware of the inner workings that will eventually emerge into a recognized point of meaning.

For us, that we may not be able to 'see' the build-up of potential may prove to be the most difficult thing to bear. Yet, it is almost common knowledge that times of seeming emptiness and lack of direction in a man's life are often just the veil over something new being brought to birth. What has worked in the past proves no longer appropriate, or a hindrance to future development. In the time of acedia, when the "spirit is dry", the old conditioning (that

was brought about by excitements and efforts) is **no longer binding and impelling**. Not that dryness or emptiness or lack of direction, in themselves, have any significance. The man must obey his inner sense of duty, doing what is necessary and avoiding what is not necessary, so that a new kind of learning and development can take place. The intelligent "seed" needs a culturing medium for its proper development, though this may have no similarities to what is significant to the man mentally or emotionally.

A famous example of this build-up of potential is in the **Curè d'Ars**, who ineffectively studied Latin for many years, in great moral suffering over his lack of ability. Yet, it was just that steadfast application and his manner of application — avoiding no evidence concerning his own stupidity and allowing no excuses to easily justify failure — that resulted in an extraordinary power of listening, from which many thousands of people drew benefit during their confessions to him.

Too often, people regard what is done rather than the manner in which it is done. Sensitivity to manner is a measure of intelligence, for it requires intelligence to know intelligence. In the same vein, these reflections cast doubts on the effectiveness of futurologists, who extrapolate trends without regard for the quality of intelligence that informs them.

no longer binding and compelling
> "Never rely upon what you believe to be inner experiences because it is only when you get beyond them that you will reach knowledge. They are there to deceive you."
> from 'Counsels of Bahaudin' in *Thinkers of the East* by Idries Shah

Curè d'Ars

"The useless efforts made by the Curè d'Ars, for long and painful years, in his attempt to learn Latin bore fruit in the marvellous discernment which enabled him to see the very soul of his penitents behind their words and even their silences."

from *Waiting on God* by Simone Weil

32. The essence of evolution

Intelligence is evolutionary. There are many useful illustrations of the workings of intelligence in the evolution of life and man. But, immediately, there is a difficulty in the way in which evolution is understood and accounted for in most current thinking. The mechanical doctrine of the "survival of the fittest" has no connection with intelligence and is deliberately opposed to an explanation in terms of intelligence. Such a doctrine has nothing to do with evolution as an ascendance to what is higher, even if only because relevance of notions of "higher" would be categorically denied by proponents of the survival doctrine. The doctrine shifts attention from the evolution of beings to their environment and interaction with the environment.

In the same way, people look for explanations of the operations of intelligence in terms of environmental influences (coupled with models of randomizing devices in the heads of men). The doctrine of the survival of the fittest makes the repository of value to be the environment, which chooses its inhabitants by inexorable mechanism. No credence is given to the possibilities of **intelligence working from within a species** to create potentialities connected with future events and with the developments of other species not immediately in spatial-temporal contact.

intelligence working from within a species

Amongst biologists, an exception is the late Sir Alister Hardy, whose book *The Living Stream* credits living beings with an intelligent influence on evolution. Konrad Lorenz, in *Behind the Mirror*, took a similar view, though expressed in different ways.

33. Role of sacrifice

Intelligence is in communication with intelligence; and the view which believes the universe to be intelligent has no difficulty in admitting intelligence incarnated into forms of life: willing, eventually, to abandon their claim of existence in favour of more suitable instruments of transformation. The laws of intelligence are as immutable as those of mechanism and conditioned existence, yet make so much mockery of ordinary thinking that the latter comes to recognise the agents of intelligence as deadly enemies.

Intelligence requires sacrifice, especially the sacrifice of false gods and illusions; a kind of sacrifice that appears, before it is taken, to demand more than the thrusting of one's arm into a flame or the giving up of life itself. Intelligence embodies a method of calculated sacrifice (**the pill of the sly man**). There is an objectivity about the costs involved in making progress.

The principle of making sacrifice is the highest order of economics. For that, which is of unknown value, the most valuable of the known must be given. Thus, all that is involved in the achievement and values of the past must be given up if the new level of achievement and new values of the future are to be realized.

pill of the sly man

"The 'sly man' knows some secret which the fakir, monk, and yogi do not know. How the 'sly man' learned this secret - it is not known. Perhaps he found it in some old books, perhaps he inherited it, perhaps he bought it, perhaps he stole it from someone. It makes no difference. The 'sly man' knows the secret and with its help outstrips the fakir, the monk, and the yogi."

"A man who follows the fourth way knows quite definitely what substances he needs for his aims and he knows that these substances can be produced within the body by a month of physical suffering, by a week of emotional strain, or a day of mental exercises - and, also, that they can be introduced into the organism from without if it is known how to do it. . . . . he [the sly man] simply prepares and swallows a little pill which contains all the substances he wants and, in this way, without loss of time, he obtains the required results."

from *In Search of the Miraculous* by P. D. Ouspensky

34. Higher and lower

That which is capable of the greatest sacrifice is the higher. This we learn in the account of Jesus Christ, the son of God, sacrificed, not to God, but to man. The account of Jesus is a message from a great intelligence, which gives us the most perfect image of the highest intelligence comprehensible to us.

In our most mundane endeavours, we instinctively know that evolution lies in the direction which costs us **not less than everything**. There is an obvious economics at the base of intelligence, the stark reality of which is rarely faced. Any evolutionary step costs us everything we have.

Of course, we learn that there is resurrection and paradise. But even paradise, again, has to be sacrificed for the sake of entrance into the higher.

The learning of sacrifice is one of the great themes of intelligence, applying equally to the great and the small.

As far as our observation of the evolution of life and man on the earth can follow, what we witness is a process in which increasing independence is given to the works of intelligence. Increasingly, intelligence is "given" to the products of intelligence until, today, a man can challenge the angels themselves, and the angels have no power of control to curb whatever comes of this — they can only appeal. Intelligence communicates with intelligence and that can be only on a basis of equality, even though there be a greater and a smaller.

not less than everything
    "Quick now, here, now, always -
    A condition of complete simplicity
    (Costing not less than everything)"
        from *Four Quartets* by T. S. Eliot

35. Originality

Intelligence is a matter of what is new in human life; but what is truly new may appear to lack originality in the eyes of those who do not see the significance of events. The originality of intelligence is an originality to be measured in terms of the whole situation. It is not simply a matter of having a new idea. The idea involved may be well-known in some applications, but only intelligence sees its potential significance in certain unthought-of-circumstances.

Similarly, a man can come to an important realization and understanding of a certain feature of human life which thousands have come to before him; but his advance is a true origination and contribution to human progress, even though it appears to influence no-one but himself.

Often enough, the glimmerings of intelligence are stifled because of romantic ideas about the nature of originality, ideas which assume that only a radically new announcement or discovery can be deemed "original". True originality is the dawn of intelligence, but to outward appearances nothing remarkable or outstanding may have happened.

36. Objectivity of purpose

Intelligence appears to have an instinct for what will prove to be significant or useful. That is because it is already in contact with the future and is taking part in the decisions which are giving the future a coherent meaning in progress. Intelligence follows invisible pathways of meaning and purpose. It is plugged into the direction of the universe and the how and why of it. The common picture of random creativity is very false. Certainly most "creative individuals" are locked inside their subjective awareness and are quite convinced they are "having ideas" or "being spontaneous"; but they fail to see the pattern to which their creativity belongs. This failure to see eventually leads to a separation from the service of intelligence and the result is a drying-up, decline or destruction.

37 Progress now

In intelligence, progress is made now. The operations of intelligence are within the present moment, but the present moment has to be large enough to enable this to happen, or open enough to enter into communication with an operative intelligence that can exert a progressive influence.

It is very important to avoid thinking of progress as a series of improvements made successively in time. **Progress** is made possible by intelligent operations working within concentrations of energy transformation that we call the present, being present and the present moment. Intelligence is free of the belief in a tomorrow in which things are achieved or realized: everything that has to be done has to be done now, or not at all.

The dimension of progress within the present is intelligence. It is aligned with neither time nor the timeless. Subjectively, it is experienced as an inner spinning or vortex that operates between the slower and the faster worlds. This spinning turns the self into a gyroscope that maintains its own stability within the flow of energies and influences.

progress

"Progress: The transition from a less to a more ordered state within a given Present Moment is the progress of that moment. Progress in one Present Moment may be at the expense of regress in another. Progress is also the way of return to the Perfectly Ordered Source."

from *The Dramatic Universe Vol. IV*
by John Bennett

38. Acceleration

Intelligence brings acceleration. It produces a shift into higher gears. Successive stages move relatively faster as penetration goes further into the dimension of progress. Acceleration is an inevitable manifestation of extension into a higher dimension. It is the outward manifestation of the same process that is inwardly manifested in "spinning".

In practice, it is difficult to distinguish between the phenomena of excited productivity and those of genuine acceleration. The former is a common legacy of having ideas, conversation, even ordinary enthusiasm. It has no necessary connection with intelligence. True acceleration is a matter of quantum jumps, discontinuities in the structure of a situation that mark an increasing rate of change towards **continuous creation**.

Change is inevitable and ordinary. It is to be expected that intelligence would manifest itself by alterations in the rate of change, since it is just that kind of alteration which lends itself to verifiable alteration. This constitutes a more primitive datum than can be provided by judgments of change in quality or level.

There are natural rates of change or rates of activities intrinsic to the construction of men and other beings. For example, there is a characteristic speed of thinking for any individual or natural grouping of human beings. Very little can be done directly to alter this basic speed. However, intelligence finds ways to bring about the effect of acceleration. Intelligence can shift into a higher gear, that is, a higher level of operation, in which connections can be made much faster. Such connections have to be reflected, eventually, in ordinary thinking; but this can be left until almost after the event of "real thinking" has concluded. People frequently comment on the evidence for the vast and incredibly speedy and accurate computational, analogical and heuristic apparatus which appears to work outside of normal consciousness. It is less frequently understood that this apparatus — which is a reflection of intelligence in the material structures of the brain, together with other physiological structures and systems of the whole body — can be engaged deliberately by putting the mental apparatus out of its lower gear and then re-engaging in a higher one. Only intelligence can change gear at will. In ordinary circumstances, such changes that do happen are a matter of accidental shocks, when the change of gear can so overwhelm the individual that he acts as if in a state of shock, with attendant personality changes. But acceleration can so alter the energy system so that normal fatigues and mechanisms of dispersal cease to have any affect.

continuous creation

"There is an optimum condition of heart, mind, soul and spirit - the state of 'metacontrol' (the sixth level of genius . . .) - in which whatever knowledge is needed floods into consciousness, CONTINUOUSLY; always completely new and without any obvious prior process of search or recall. You will know when you are making real progress with your own inner development when you break through, increasingly, into this 'living knowledge'."

from *The Road to True Professionalism* by Edward Matchett

39. Reality of diversity

The computational aspect of the higher gears involves radical changes in quality as well as quantity: vastly different kinds of data can be instantaneously scanned and processed, instead of data artificially reduced to being of the same kind, which is the way of working of the ordinary mind. Thus, for example, the ordinary mind may treat values as if they were material facts; or even if a proper distinction is made, that is where it ends: with data from the two realms kept apart in rigid apartheid. For the ordinary mind, there is no way of computing with facts and values together without reducing something of the essential nature of either or both. In intelligence, however, computation accommodates both kinds of data. This is not surprising, since an essential work of intelligence is in the realization of value in material circumstances.

Similarly, intelligence is equally at home with fiction and actuality. It can operate with data from either of the two domains; and, while retaining all that is essential of the distinction between them, can see behind their obvious distinctions to an inner unity and mutual relevance. This claim is substantiated by the work of every great historian and every important novelist or writer. Is the reality of Greece in the archaeology of stones or in the plays of Aeschylus and Sophocles? "Greece was the cradle of Western Civilization" is a fiction that has served well for more than a thousand years and now needs to be challenged. The more meaningful account must be more accurate as well as a more effective stimulus to the imagination of people.

The accommodation of intelligence to a wider, more diverse universe of information gives it powers vastly superior to ordinary mentation. In this way, it is fairly easy to see that intelligence can make rapid strides, whereas thinking would plod slowly. The more the degrees of freedom, the higher the dimension of thought and the more inevitable manifestations of acceleration.

40. Control of complexity

One of the signs of progress is deepening control over complexity; a control that does not work by the reduction and elimination of the complexities, but by progressive integration. More and more independent centers of meaning are gathered together for mutual enhancement and significance; multifarious planes of thought, action and decision develop and transform into each other. Wider and wider orders of freedom in strategy and tactics emerge. These things do not happen a step at a time but are a process of enrichment from within the present moment. The important choices to be made are to be made now.

Awareness of the association of progress with mastery over complexity has led many people to explore and develop techniques and ideas for enlarging the complexity-capacity of the mind. The instruments so involved are often themselves expressions of intelligence, but they are also often taken to be the very substance of the intelligence that produced them — instead of the shell. The important difference is that intelligence leads a man to the point at which he can begin to see the inner decisions and commitments he is called upon to make in order to make progress in his own situation. This includes making progress in his encounter with complexity. A certain skill and understanding is involved, too, because simple mind-stretching by involvement in complex information may make use of only a part of the energy apparatus available for the purposes of self-evolution and hence, progress in mastery over **complexity**.

Finally, intelligence forms its own "intelligence-event" or present moment. Subjective experience may display the event in separate periods of activity; but some individuals are able to recognize that what happens is a periodic re-entry into the same event, recognizable by its distinctive qualities and its "spinning".

complexity

> "All existence presents itself to us as an organised complexity. We ourselves are no exception to this rule. Every attempt to give an account of human nature in simple terms is bound to fail, because our complexity is the very condition of being what we are."
>
> from *The Dramatic Universe* Vol. III by John Bennett

41. Chaos and destruction

Intelligence has a strange alliance with chaos and destruction. In reviewing human history, we can find countless examples of progress being made in the aftermath of failure and destruction: the blending of East and West that came after the vicious and brutal carnage of the Mongols; the dissolution of the power of monarchy in Europe after the seeming failure of the 1848 revolutions; the emergence of Christianity after the moral disintegration of Rome. While most men remain hypnotized by power and ordinary criteria of success and failure, others see deeper strata of significance in the course of events and achieve their results without fighting against the inevitable.

42. Non-violence

Often enough, old forms or authorities need to be destroyed; but intelligence itself cannot take up a sword and bring about their ruin. In time, force and falsity bring about, by themselves, self-destruction through revolt or an apathy that leads to vulnerability to external forces. In those moments, it is possible for intelligence to intervene and make use of the situation, harnessing the forces of change according to its own vision of what is needed in the future. Intelligence does not achieve results by force or resistance to force. People involved in producing change too often involve themselves in applying forces to situations that, inevitably, generate their own counter-forces or reactions. It is one of the insights of intelligence that violence in any form does not work.

In our complex tasks, intelligence is always recognizable as the "something else" that is neither for nor against the authorities or systems that belong to the situation. It can operate in such a way that it appears to have no relevance to the "major issues" involved. For that reason, it is often ignored and left to do its work unmolested, even in the heat of a bitter struggle.

While most people shudder at chaos and destruction, intelligence seeks out the meaningful possibilities that are brought into being. Intelligence can take advantage of the stress and partial de-conditioning undergone by people in a time of trouble. The biggest enemy of intelligence is not strife but complacency. Intelligence makes sense in a troubled world!

43. Specificity of sensitivities

Almost as an aside, it is useful to remember the traditional teaching concerning the nature of ordinary thinking, namely, that it is of the same nature as that of **material objects**. This state of affairs has advantages in that thinking can exactly mirror in itself the properties and operations of material objects and thus give rise to technology. But it has disadvantages in rendering the mind insensitive to the phenomena of living things and human relations. The consequent disasters are visible at every hand in the way we run our affairs.

Intelligence is the reverse to ordinary thinking; intelligence can operate only by speaking with the intelligence of what it is concerned with. Specific channels of sensitivity open corresponding to the true nature of what is "studied". There are as many channels as there are "species".

material objects

> "Inanimate matter, which appears to be without any power of
> its own, has in reality a most potent force of attraction
> because, in its essential qualities, it corresponds to the quality
> of human thought."

from *Susila Budhi Dharma* by Muhammad Subuh

44. Discrimination

It can happen that intelligence accelerates past the individual himself and he has to wait a long period of time before the next step
appears to him. Intelligence is time-travel. It can answer such questions as: "What would I say to my present self if I were speaking from
the vantage point of the next minute, hour, day, year?".

One of the most powerful images ever made for the depiction of
intelligence was Maxwell's "Demon", the infinitesimal creature who
could open a door to let fast molecules travel in one direction and
slow in the opposite direction, thereby generating a temperature difference that could lead to the performance of work. Intelligence is
the small that matters.

Many clever people bent their efforts to proving that the Demon
would generate as much entropy in its activities as would be lost by
the unmixing of the slow and the fast. The point of the Demon,
however, is not to defeat the laws of materiality and time on their
own plane of operation, but to introduce into that plane an operation which is not dependent on those laws. In this case, the key element is discrimination.

An intelligent man can change his own being by allowing only
fine-quality impressions to enter him. This he will achieve by work on
his attention and emotionality so that in every event the perception
of what is highest is most favored. He will not achieve it by attempt-
ing to separate himself from experiences he arbitrarily labels as "bad".

In the world of materiality, intelligence does not "do" anything, merely discriminates and separates using the energies and forces available.

Discrimination in a man is the seed of intelligence in him. Every genuine act of distinguishing higher from lower — or any kind of real distinction — is an act of intelligence. But the man himself has to make that act, or realize that act. It is a totally different situation to be involved in classification, especially according to labels attached by other people.

"I distinguish" is the first and the essential act of human intelligence, more fundamental than "I name" or "I know". Even then, the act of distinguishing may take place outside of awareness, leaving its results to gradually emerge into a meaningful picture or image "in the mind".

It is only through genuine distinguishing that a man can attain self-control: if he cannot distinguish higher from lower, he is adrift and has no fulcrum of control and no means of making effective decisions.

45. Substantiality

Intelligence has its own substantiality. It is not devoid of materiality, since it is involved in the emergence of form and experience. Intelligence can control the transformation of energies. There is a mode of intelligence that converts "food" into "thinking"; and another, by which a man can turn his thinking into useful work.

Intelligence operates in the realm of superimposed controls in human culture in the form of psychological insights and methods that enable people to attain a real insight into their own nature and what is required of them. Such controls cannot be widely spread since they, too, are material and hence of finite capacity.

Cathedrals, poems, ideas are points of concentration of intelligent energy of control. Usually, every man who bears intelligence creates his own form of concentration. It may be in doing one thing well. It always involves being able to perform a whole task, carrying things through to completion, bearing all the risks and developing all the needed skills for himself.

46. Love and evil

Intelligence without love is evil. **Evil** is the "sufficient unto itself". Only love is higher than intelligence and by submission to this higher value, intelligence can be saved from itself. Intelligence is not capable of love by means of its own transformations and operations; love is something else.

Love should proceed intelligence and intelligence should give way to love. Love is what is impossible for intelligence; love goes outside the laws under which intelligence must operate. In love, all things are equal; whereas in intelligence, there must be discrimination and choice, higher and lower, and the rejection of the not useful.

By one of those peculiar human inversions, the idea of love often leads to a non-intelligent passivity and meekness. This is an exact inversion, since it puts love below intelligence instead of above. All men of great intelligence come to the point at which it is realized that "Love is the Real Impossible".

evil

"...the source of evil is an Intelligence, limited and not Divine...we can ascribe the Fall of Man to the jealousy of the powers that were charged with endowing him with creativity..."

from *The Dramatic Universe* Vol. IV by John Bennett

47 Authentic wholeness

Intelligence is an operation of the Whole; it is not the addition of another part. In most situations, people do not know what the Whole of the situation is. Therefore, they attempt to operate and think in terms of systems, models and beliefs which deal in only partial aspects; and, often, they believe that such partial endeavours can be added together to find the "Whole thing". But true integration can work only if it stems from the Whole to start with. And if that condition applies, then every partial aspect will be developed as an expression of the Whole and the need for integration will no longer exist.

The Whole is essentially in every true part of the Whole, the true part is not "apart" but "participates".

48. Heaven and earth

The Whole of a situation is the "Kingdom of Heaven" of the situation; and like the Kingdom of Heaven, is with us now if we could cross the barrier in our own natures that divides us. The Kingdom is not in some other place or time, although it is "yet to come" when intelligence has not yet progressed to enable it to be **the present**.

the present
Hyparchic Future (also Past and Present):

"A region of experience in which the Will is free from the limitations of existence and yet can operate to produce transformations. Has the characteristics of the Future, except that it is free from all pre-determination. Equated to the 'Kingdom of Heaven'. The same condition can also be experienced within the present moment (ecstasy or transformation), and can remain in the Past (the Living Past)."

from *The Dramatic Universe* Vol. IV by John Bennett

49. The unanswered question

Intelligence indicates to us our lack of it, which is how we begin to become intelligent. It is the lamp casting light on the page, revealing the words we do not understand. It enables us to become puzzled and ask questions for which there is no grammar. Finally, we reach for the pen and begin to write — because there is no alternative.

The Unanswered Question
>   The title of one of the most remarkable compositions by Charles Ives, the American twentieth century composer. Quiet strings represent the background of the cosmos. A trumpet asks 'the' question, calmly and clearly; but then the human voices echo the question, breaking into discord as no answer comes - in the form that they expect.

50. Media

When something is achieved, it may appear as the consequence of controlled effort applied to recalcitrant material. But, it is also the case that intelligence has communicated with intelligence and come to an agreement with itself. The meaning of intelligence is not simply in construction but also in concurrence. Intelligence fabricates signposts and "receivers"; the one to indicate where it may be found and the other to provide a means of hearing it. Every new invention is a kind of "listening post", at which we may eavesdrop on the continuing **dialogue**.

dialogue

According to David Bohm, the word 'dialogue' does not mean conversation between two people but derives from: dia or 'through' and logos or 'meaning' (cf. *On Dialogue* by David Bohm). One of the leading ideas of dialogue is that there is a whole of which we, as separate people with our own belief systems, agendas and personalities, see only a part. Coming together in dialogue gives us a chance of seeing the whole. To do this, we must learn how to preserve all the diversity and differences we can from amongst us. There are various stages in this process, though they may happen at various times. Amongst the myriad of possibilities, here are some, according to the principles of *N-logue*:

Monalogue: everyone can speak their mind without interruption, so that a shared picture of the whole builds up, a 'monad', uncluttered by pet theories, slogans, quoting authorities, etc.

Dyalogue: this is where an issue is highlighted in an exchange between two participants who have quite contrasting views and challenge each other to go more deeply.

Trialogue: this is where there is a generation of new ideas in the moment, which usually turns out to involve three people, though not always the same ones as the action unfolds.

from *Structures of Meaning* by Anthony Blake

51. The Speaking Part

Who is there to describe **intelligence**? And by what can it be described?

intelligence

> "The Wisdom [Sophia] that played before the Lord' was not the Creation being made, it was somehow the creative imagination. . . .
>
> "For me it becomes more and more sure, as I live with it, that there is this power of creative imagination that has all these properties: making doing possible, rejoicing before the Lord, giving the power to see through the inner eye, and working in all nature, accompanying the whole process of the appearance and creation of life on this Earth for a thousand million years.
>
> "There would be no way of coming to the oneness of mankind, if we were always dependent upon angels being sent to do things. It is more intimate than that."
>
> from *Sacred Influences* by John Bennett

52. Is mankind intelligent?

Intelligence cannot be counted and turned into numbers. There are not a number of intelligences. The intelligent person is only a semblance of intelligence. Human beings are inadequate as models of what intelligence is but have appeared on Earth to bring the question into focus.

Can the intelligence of mankind be increased or bettered? But, from where shall intelligence be gathered and who can combine the parts together? To what can intelligence be attached? We know that people need to be alive, thus, looking after the body is intelligent. Whenever people are treated more intelligently, they then become more intelligent themselves. This is a transaction deeper than marriage and one obscured by education; it is the most important work there is and therefore the most neglected. It is the discovery of the "fittest" in an intelligent way and not through random exposure to life's disasters of death and starvation. Otherwise, the best course would be to lock people into a cage to fight it out, or pit them against each other in the stock exchange; in other words, to act as mankind currently conducts itself: through violence and greed. To treat another intelligently is to speak to their intelligence and not to tell them what to do or think, which means: to lose one's power over them. Just at the point where such abstinence teeters on the verge of foolish vulnerability, a door is opened. It is something impossible to calculate, wonderful to behold, and unnoticed by the multitude. Even the greatest art barely approaches this condition, or the world would have been long enlightened. But, for all that, art is intelligent in its praise of folly, its articulation of speechlessness, its understanding of misunderstanding, and its fulfilment of unknown longings.

53. Concentration

Does intelligence require a body or an engine? If there is to be an effect, then the means must be there. A means is something that concentrates what is otherwise dispersed or fragmented, such as: a handbag or a lens, a brain or a sail, a poem or an organism, a house or a theoretical principle, a leaf or a star. In concentrating, a means comes into relation with other means, a body with other bodies. It also comes into relation with itself, which is why it might appear intelligent. Without concentration, there can be no effect of intelligence.

Concentration is a consequence of the many in their diversity. Intelligence diversifies diversity and concentrates concentration and everything thus appears as bodies and engines. Concentration comes from intelligence and leads to intelligence. Thus, evolution is intelligent and must diversify the diverse as much as it unifies the singular.

54. Design

Intelligence is reflected in its own productions, which makes it appear that these productions give rise to it. Thus, it is that men appear intelligent and their works capable also of intelligence. All intelligence is artificial because it is a work of design. It is in the media common to "designer" and "designed", whereby these two can be articulated without disjunction. There is not a source of intelligence in time and space. It does not come from anywhere. It is being put into effect by its own works. The "argument from design" supposed that the organization of the universe demonstrated a "creator". However, what it does is to suggest design or intelligence. All creators, agents and organisms are discovered in the medium of intelligence, that is, in the work of design. The most important feature of the universe is that it is being designed by itself. It does not simply "go on" nor does it merely "obey laws". The designer is within the design and has to invent himself in order to do anything. Therefore, the purpose and intelligence of the universe appear to us as fictions.

design

In a story recounted by Idries Shah, a Naqshbandi was asked to explain the meaning of their name "The Designer". The Sufi tells a story of tinsmith's escape from prison, who says afterwards:

"It is a matter of design and design within design. My wife is a weaver. She found the man who had made the locks of the cell door and got the design from him. This she wove into the carpet, at the spot where my head touched in prayer five times a day. I am a metal-worker, and this design looked to me like the inside of a lock. I designed the plan of the artefacts to obtain the materials to make the key - and I escaped."

55. Perfection

In this sense, intelligence has to do with absolute perfection, and with the fulfillment of the command of Jesus: "Be ye perfect, even as your Father which is in Heaven". This impossible command was meant, and is to be taken, seriously. There is no point at all in being imperfect; and intelligence will not rest with anything less than perfection. In fact, intelligence loathes imperfection and in this loathing may be its chief weakness, which necessitates its dependence on love: that intelligence is as capable of destroying the imperfect as it is in creating the perfect.

Perfection is not intended here to mean the opposite of actuality. Perfection encompasses actuality and is real. To perfect means to carry to completion. In perfection, earth becomes a true part of heaven; the part becomes a particle of the Whole.

56. Stupidity

As long as you ignore what is being said here, you have a chance of understanding it.

Yes, we have to make efforts. But, that is only to show that they miss the point. Try to understand this. Reading difficult books is also preferred over eliminating stupidity.

Intelligence shines through everything as if it were not there. This makes it unpopular with people who want to cast their own shadows. Who would want to be a window when one can be a door! Stupidity seems to be a more convincing proof of one's existence than intelligence. So, we keep our door shut just in case!

What can we do about stupidity? Nothing — we have done too much already.

C O D A

ACTION IS INTELLIGENT ONLY

WHEN WHATEVER IS

GOING ON CAN BE

STOPPED

NOW

Gerald Wilde & Intelligence Now

Gerald Wilde (1905 - 1986) was one of the most outstanding British painters of this century but largely unrecognised save by fellow artists and some leading critics, such as David Sylvester, who writes: "Violent and vertiginous, the paintings have a feeling of chaos faced, all but embraced, and somehow held at bay. It is an art which has the exhilaration of a disaster just averted."

Intelligence Now was painted in response to the idea of this book and now hangs in the October Gallery, London. Marie Harding writes about it:

"Wilde's quest engaged him in the rigorous exploration of the structures of thought. If a painting cannot be read, it is of no consequence. *Intelligence Now*, one of his recurrent themes, captures a new form: a brain-like shape with all the inner pathways revealed, it is a two dimensional piece suggesting multi-dimensional access floating in space. Lines curving, networking, he breaks beyond Western logic and illustrates the practicality of non-linear thinking in the space and information age."

from *Gerald Wilde (1905-1986)*, edited by Chili Hawes

Edward Matchett (1929-1998)
written by John Kirby

Edward Matchett was born in Nottinghamshire in the heart of England in 1929. He was a true self taught genius whose generosity of spirit is shown by his unceasing quest to develop this genius in all he came into contact with.

Between 1960 –1970, as well as qualifying as an engineer, he also taught at the Engineering Employer's Management School at Bristol, subsequently working and teaching in Argentina, followed by time in Italy at the United Nations Organization Vocational Training Centre in Turin, and for 3 years in the Pilkington Laboratories in England, as well as other work for industry and governments.

In the mid 1960s he was given a five year grant by the Science Research Council of Great Britain to look into ways of cultivating genius within the UK to combat the imminent threat from Japan to the UK's manufacturing industry. It was during this time that he contributed major breakthroughs in the form of his Fundamental Design Method (FDM), and by the end of the 1960s his core 3M discipline, 'the making of media plus matter meaningful in time delta-t', where media is put first as the non-material energy in which is all that is and all that could be. Matter is understood not just as the material universe we can touch and see but also thoughts, memories and experiences. Time ∂t refers to the instant, the moment, when contact is made with media, which is outside of linear time. The content, the input for that moment, is complete for that moment itself, the next moment may be an entirely new situation with entirely different contact. "This is the secret of genius: putting to use not intellect alone...but rather all that one has been, seen, felt, intuited and known at first hand throughout the entire process of living. 'Making media plus matter meaningful in time ∂t' is a channelling of the whole of life's experiences into each new moment of endeavour, and doing this primarily through just letting it happen. It is the most natural process available to you, though it is frequently one that has been blocked and inhibited since your very first taste of formal education....It is not a process that need be at enmity with the scientific method or with true education." (*From Talent to Genius*, Edward Matchett).

At the core of all that he did was a deep and lifelong religious faith. For the last ten years of his life his main focus was on the final stage of his work which he called Sophiagenics. Grounded in the 3M discipline, Sophiagenics ('the acquiring of wisdom') rests on the promise and fruit of Pentecost that the Holy Spirit, from which all media emanates, will empower, guide and protect all those who sincerely invite him to do so. It is a universal discipline accessible to all through which a person can develop not only intimacy with the Holy Spirit, but through the applied moment by moment discipline, can also be empowered and informed regarding any situation. Edward Matchett considered Sophiagenics to be vastly more important than any of his other work. Edward Matchett died on 1st December 1998.

Anthony Blake

He studied physics at Bristol University, where he was taught by David Bohm, and the History and Philosophy of Science at Cambridge. He practised the Gurdjieff system under John Bennett and became one of his collaborators in the development of *Systematics* and *Structural Communication*, as well as an assistant in Bennett's experimental 'school' of rapid holistic learning, or *Continuous Education*. He collaborated with John Allen on the development of the idea of *biospherics* and with Edward Matchett on the release of creative intelligence, especially through *Neural Education (ILM)*. He studied the *Laws of Form* with Spencer Brown and worked on the meaning of *Dialogue* with the School of Ignorance.

He is the author of *A Seminar on Time, Studies on Systems, Structures of Meaning, The Intelligent Enneagram, Perspectives, Enneagrams* and others; is editor of *Future Management* and the originator of the *DuVersity*. He has written science fiction. He is working on a series of video-dialogues with original thinkers who can speak in the moment called *Conversations from the Emerging World*.

A teacher and explorer of transformational methods, he specialises in structural thinking and dialogue, extending the work of Bennett, Bohm and others. He is presently working on new forms of communication, called *N-logue*, and ways of accessing cognitive alternatives such as *ILM*. One of his projects is to find a rational way of understanding higher intelligence. He runs seminars in the USA and Europe, often as collaborations with other independent thinkers and artists.

Married to a Finn, Anna-Lisa Eivor, he has six children — George, David, William, Edmund, Cosmo and Victoria — and lives in the Borders of Scotland.

Twelve Hypotheses of Higher Intelligence

Here is a sketch of perspectives on the theme of higher intelligence. Our understanding of communication with higher intelligence must depend on our view of what such intelligence 'is'.

A. The first group concerns the hypothesis of higher intelligence as a human potential.
   1. The hypothesis of a higher faculty. A varied group of ideas, though largely clustered around the two concepts of (a) conscience (moral order and will), and (b) intuition (direct perception, intelligence). It is proposed that accessing such faculties can make our intelligence higher (more moral, or more high powered) (Gurdjieff).
   2. The hypothesis of exceptional people, or genius. In this hypothesis, the assumption is made that an active intelligence is embodied in a few people. It is sometimes avowed that what we need most is the cultivation and utilization of genius (Matchett).
   3. The hypothesis of co-operative intelligence. In this, it is proposed that, if and when, people 'coalesce' their individual intelligences, then a higher order can emerge. One avenue of this approach is through dialogue methods, etc. (Bohm)
   4. The combined hypothesis of a special group of people (still basically human) in whom higher intelligence is embodied. This is the assertion of a 'hidden directorate', or hidden masters, who influence human affairs through 'sensitive' intermediaries. Along with this may be added the postulate of an intrinsic social order of intelligence (Bennett).

B. The second group postulates an independent class of entities as the higher intelligence.
   5. The hypothesis of the noosphere. In this hypothesis, it is proposed that the natural evolution of the planet produces a realm

of intelligence that has independent existence from that of the human population. Hence, that there is an 'Overmind' or some such, arising out of physical laws (Vernadsky).

6. The hypothesis of supernatural intelligence. In this hypothesis, there is an underlying assertion of supernatural agency involved in evolution. We note here the two-fold form this takes (see 1 above) in terms of the 'angels' or 'messengers' and the 'demiurge' or the 'workers' (Bennett).

7. The hypothesis of extraterrestrial higher intelligence. The higher intelligence is ascribed to beings of other planetary systems, usually belonging to other solar systems.

8. The combined hypothesis of planetary destiny, in which it is proposed that every planet with life has an ordained destiny differing from any other.

C. The last group of hypotheses concerns intelligence as 'hidden in time'.

9. The hypothesis of the ancestral wisdom. This ancient hypotheses ascribes wisdom or higher intelligence to the corpus of the ancestors, from whom we may receive guidance (Shamanism).

10. The hypothesis of intelligence as belonging to the future. In this hypothesis, higher intelligence is positioned in the future, through the future of a special kind (Tipler). For example, in a crossover concept between hypotheses, some explain 'extra-terrestrial intelligence' as we ourselves 'coming from the future'.

11. The hypothesis of higher intelligence as the fastest rate of becoming, and belonging to the present instant. This is the rarest form of belief in higher intelligence.

12. The combined hypothesis of higher intelligence as time itself. (Zurvanism). In this hypothesis, an attempt is made to combine all other hypotheses and begin from a starting point that does not distinguish human forms of intelligence from others.

D. What remains

There is an open area concerning the 'fact' that higher intelligence is itself limited and supposes a higher order still. In this, we might also consider that our very idea of 'higher' might be called into question. Many evolutionary biologists say that we cannot even call human intelligence 'higher' than that of any other species. There is a thirteenth hypothesis! This hypothesis can serve as a new starting point.

There are three main areas of denial of higher intelligence, of very different kinds.

1. There are no differences in level between any one form of organized intelligence and another. This is because intelligence is taken as relative to the goals or type of 'intentionality' of the given entity.

2. There cannot be any higher intelligence because there is nothing intermediary between man and God. All that is higher than human intelligence is beyond reason altogether and totally divine and unknowable.

3. Intelligence is a property of language and manifests only when there are communicating systems. Intelligence is not a property of any class of being. Alternatively, that: language itself is higher intelligence (Vico, Joyce).

From such bases, it is probable possible to generate a further set of twelve hypotheses representing the 'shadow' or negative side of the former set. Each such set of hypotheses might be taken as a complex worldview; and we might proceed to generate cycles of worldviews, of indeterminate number.